ADELAIDE LITERARY AWARD
2018

ADELAIDE
LITERARY AWARD
ANTHOLOGY
2018

POETRY

Adelaide Books
New York/Lisbon
2018

ADELAIDE LITERARY AWARD 2018
POETRY ANTHOLOGY
Special Issue of the Adelaide Literary Magazine

September 2018

ISBN-13: 978-1-949180-56-5
ISBN-10: 1-949180-56-5

Adelaide Literary Magazine is an independent international monthly publication, based in New York and Lisbon. Founded by Stevan V. Nikolic and Adelaide Franco Nikolic in 2015, the magazine's aim is to publish quality poetry, fiction, nonfiction, artwork, and photography, as well as interviews, articles, and book reviews, written in English and Portuguese. We seek to publish outstanding literary fiction, nonfiction, and poetry, and to promote the writers we publish, helping both new, emerging, and established authors reach a wider literary audience. We publish print and digital editions of our magazine twelve times a year. Online edition is updated continuously. There are no charges for reading the magazine online.
(http://adelaidemagazine.org)

EDITOR IN CHIEF
Stevan V. Nikolic
editor@adelaidemagazine.org

MANAGING DIRECTOR
Adelaide Franco Nikolic

GRAPHIC & WEB DESIGN
Joana Cardoso
Vesna Trpkovska

Published by: Adelaide Books LLC, New York
244 Fifth Avenue, Suite D27, New York, NY 10001
e-mail: info@adelaidebooks.org
phone: 917 477 8984

Best poems by the Winner, seven Shortlist Nominees
and fifty Finalists of the second annual
Adelaide Literary Award Competition 2018,
selected by

Stevan V. Nikolic

editor-in-chief

Content

THE WINNER

Museum

The meadow spoke as the oldest wood from the museum,
wild flowers, opened in pollens and
bursting as the fullest buds,
I walked so gingerly.

The blades of the grassy spears lanced to the thickness
of the lowering sky. I dipped my way
through the descending fog;
cottons stretched across me.

The earth moaned in a hush as I stepped upon
the soil and buried rocks.

I looked to the cloak of the sun and reached the green pond,
filled with kelp and thick films.

The meadow came to pass thousands
of rotations around the sun.
I forever rest upon this gripping dance
beneath the descending fog.

Donny Barilla, a poet covering the realms: human intimacy, nature, mythology, theology, and man's relationship with death and the departed, has been writing for over three decades. He writes daily and strives to renew himself as an artist from page to page and body of work to body of work. Very seldom does he take a break from writing as he views it as a full-time job. He lives a reclusive lifestyle and finds himself clinging close to nature and all her elements. His home state of Pennsylvania strikes chords of poetic depth about him as he finds loveliness from cornfield to meadow. Whether it's feelings of love, intimacy, or a special closeness, he maintains the feeling that death does not take these with him/her to the grave. Emotions and feeling outlast the flesh of the human body. Human intimacy draws near an enigmatic spiritual passion which conquers all on the prismatic scale of experience. When speaking of mythology Donny says, "myths were created to make sense of feelings which are complicated by very nature. They are perhaps more easily understood through persons greater than oneself. As for theology, a disciplined aspect, incorporates quite finely with passions and secured poetic comforts.

SHORTLIST WINNER NOMINEES

All-American Competition

by Idalis Nieves

One winner to be chosen in the end
Two opposing teams on the battlefield
Three subject matters to discuss
Four hours on television to look your best
Five million eyes watching your every move
Six times spent learning the play-by-play

Six people you specifically watch attention from
One chance or you blow it
Two million screams of delight and disgust
Five hundred dollar ensemble
To be fitted for
Seven magazine shoots to attend

One motivating pep talk
Two thumbs up
Three unfaltering cartoon strips of you
A state of the union
Address to deliver
Hundreds of neighbors to impress

Five out of ten people
Looking into the contenders
One contender looking to cheat
Their way into victory
Six feet under in false promises
Zero ways to get out

A thousand ways to derail the situation
A voice of common sense lost
Tens of millions of people
Ignorant to their surroundings
Three out of four media stations in favor
Of you

One heart lost in competition
Two inner voices talking to you
Three close calls in the media
Four years to prove yourself
Five years spent building you up
Six million to be angered and disappointed

One major mistake realized, two sides to
Each story, four to six months spent in court,
Twelve people deciding your fate, two lives that have been led

Idalis Nieves, class of 2018 of Linfield College, uses her degree in Creative Writing to tell stories and that ring true to her as well as those around her. Additionally, she has had two blog entries published on empowerteen.org, a website and organization known for hosting workshops for preteen and teen girls who face challenges such as bullying, relationship troubles, and trying to find themselves. No matter what, Idalis finds a way to make her words appeal to a wide audience.

Blood Moon

by Robert René Galván

The blood moon hangs
Like a drop of amber oil,
Waxes over a stand
Of grey towers
Where a grove
Of locusts once stood:

The habitation of the bear
And speckled fawns,
A stream of trout,
And long before,
The range of immense beasts
Whose stride shook
The ground amid
Giant dragonflies
And enormous ferns –

All unfurled
From diatoms
And acrid pools
Into the tree of life,

The red orb,
A witness,
Tethered
To the world
Like a lonely atom,
Even as it melts
Into rings.

Robert René Galván, born in San Antonio, resides in New York City where he works as a professional musician and poet. He has taught at Manhattan College, The College of Mount Saint Vincent and the Brooklyn Conservatory of Music. His last collection of poems is entitled, Meteors, published by Lux Nova Press. His poetry was recently featured in Adelaide Literary Magazine, Right Hand Pointing and will appear in the Fall 2018 issue of Hawaii Review and the Winter 2018 issue of UU World.

Seascape

by Rita Baker

Forward, pounding, breaking waves.
Back retreating, meeting waves.
Like a mountain riding high,
Rolling and arched against the sky,
It's back again towards the shore,
Repeating rhythms as before.
All blue and green and foaming white,
Exiting with its powerful might.
Then further on along the beach,
Where width limits the water's reach,
It inches its way up the sand
To hurry back from the land.
A ritual dance performed with grace
Hugging the shore in quick embrace.
Like a bond you cannot sever,
An affair that lasts forever.
One moment heaving beating wild,
Next moment gently swaying mild.
A fury when wind whipped and blown.
Calm peaceful when left alone.

"I've been writing since the age of five when I discovered the magic of words. At first, fairy tales, and as I grew so my stories grew with me. Then came poetry, a love that has never left me. But it was when my children left home and I found time to write my first novel that I felt complete. As far back as I can remember, there was a nagging inside me to write. The nagging didn't let go until I had written the first line of the first page of a novel. We don't always discover who we are, or who we are meant to be, but when we do, there is no feeling more wonderful or more fulfilling."

The Hypocrite

by Lauren Bush

I am the vain looker-on who, when faced by this
house of mirrors, seeks tirelessly for my own
reflection in the impenetrable glass—an
inoperative window obscured by breath.
I am the hypocrite who sings of solitude,
yet still I yearn for an Other…
be it not death, earth's intimate lover,
then let it be a mirror of flesh and blood.
I am the poet who holds three dwellings:
Language, time, and the inconsequential skin of things.
I am the bearer of an abortive truth.
I am a false prophet promised oblivion.
A lifeless eternity hangs in my breath,
and still, I choose to exhale. My sighs—in
silence—affirm my fleeting existence,
and bring the eternal air to tremble.
Translucent hands hold my Self from my Being,
so that I may look with undiscerning eyes upon a
heap of broken images, which all of
eternity is still too fleeting to capture.
My existence beckons an upheaval of

truth, so that I may attempt to transform it,
to seal it away in my voiceless heart,
only to speak of it too soon…
I am the hypocrite.
I sing of my ignorance,
of this tragic comportment,
this abysmal dwelling…
I am the fool who affirms ambiguity,
and negates eternally present time.
I watch the sun drip over the horizon each day,
impatient for a reality, longing for fate…
I am the endless poem beginning.
I am the abyss; in flesh and blood, I am living.
This is my prison, I've confirmed, and here I will rise
again, and again, and again…

Lauren Elizabeth Bush is a student at Washington University in St.Louis. She is studying Neuropsychology and Germanic Languages and Literature.

The End Is Song

by Dr. Peter Scheponik

Walking the dog this morning,
I came upon a dragon fly
lying on the concrete way,
on its back, legs moving—
slow motion in air.
Though it seemed like it wanted
to turn over and fly away,
legs folding and unfolding,
it simply remained there.
It was a young dragon
whose cellophane wings were so clear
they seemed to disappear in the pavement.
The insect was dying.
The slow fact of its passing
pressed into my mind.
In the great universal scheme of life,
the death of a single dragon fly
doesn't seem like much.
But watching it releasing itself—
or watching it being released from this world—

touched something so deep in me.
As if Fate had led me to this place,
as if Earth had whispered in a voice
made of grace,
delicate as a dragonfly's wing:
"Look and see, my observant friend.
This…this is how it is done.
This is how you sing the end."

P.C. Scheponik is a lifelong poet who lives by the sea with his wife, Shirley, and their shizon, Bella. His writing celebrates nature, the human condition, and the metaphysical mysteries of life. He has published four collections of poems: Psalms to Padre Pio (National Centre for Padre Pio, INC), A Storm by Any Other Name and Songs the Sea has Sung in Me (PS Books, a division of Philadelphia Stories), and And the Sun Still Dared to Shine (Mazo Publishers). His work has also appeared in numerous literary journals, among them, Adelaide, Visitant, Red Eft Review, Boned, Time of Singing, WINK and others.

The Attic

by Edward Bonner

Up the creaky stained dried attic stairs.
Hidden words become a dreamer's delight.

A single forty watt incandescent bulb emits a three-
dimensional shadow, only the bravest human will investigate.

Dust particles float between the sun's rays and the dark abyss.
Unpublished covert files,
tablets,
binders and literature,
a forgotten maker of reality.

Boxes full of things we might need,
pots and pans, antique glass ware, clothing.
Games like Monopoly, Parcheesi and checkers.
All waiting to come out of hibernation.

Even a good few strands of silk gathered
spider webs hang from the rafters.

Only to give us a miniature tantrum
when they cling to our face.

Swatting, batting and slashing away the sticky goo,
crying out the spider may be crawling on you.
Finally reaching the lone cedar chest.
Positioned in the middle of the room.

I see the past,
I see the present.
I see the future.

Everything is connected,
all part of a whole.

Life is full of ups and downs for us to understand.
Our choice is to follow.

Edward Bonner grew up in a small mill town in Pittsburgh Pennsylvania. Hazelwood, Pa. A very rough neighborhood. Raised by his mother and grandparents until he was 13 years old. That's when his mother remarried. He then moved to a suburb south of Pittsburgh. Growing up, he probably got into trouble like most kids. An avid outdoorsman. 5th degree black belt / 36 years in Shotokan karate. Author of "One Kiss" Just One Kiss. A collection of love poems and more. Author of Through The Eyes Of A Lost Boy. A collection of poetry about "Love, Loss, Trauma, Pain and Healing. A journey of life through writing.

Rapunzel

by Debbie Richard

Her prison was not a round brick tower
like the one in the fairy-tale,
but a bedroom in the upstairs of a house
where a window overlooked the grounds –
green, lush, inviting.
A Tyrant, no less, oversaw her existence
with rarely a word of kindness,
most often sharply spoken words
meant to keep her oppressed.
This maiden's blond hair, too, had
been cut short, leaving her without
a means of escape.

Debbie Richard is listed in the Directory of Poets & Writers as both a poet and creative nonfiction writer. Her poem, "Between Two Worlds," was selected as Adelaide Voices Literary Award for Poetry FINALIST for 2018. Her poems have appeared in Torrid Literature Journal, Adelaide Literary Magazine, Scarlet Leaf Review, WestWard Quarterly, Halcyon Days, and others. A chapbook of poetry entitled "Resiliency," was published in 2012 by Finishing Line Press. "Hills of Home," a memoir about growing up in Appalachia, was released in 2014 by eLectio Publishing. Her current project, a full-length volume of poetry entitled "PIVOT," illustrated by the award-winning artist/illustrator, Ashley Teets, has an expected release date of December 2018 by Adelaide Books of New York. www.debbierichard.com

FINALISTS

Winter

By Anwar G. Jaber

A Grey Winter

Winter is a cruel knife cuts my joints with a cold blood. He isn't smiling; he is grey just like my dream. This winter which I feel vigorously is not kind, and you can see the sad tears in its pocket. His rain colors my soul with pale smiles and his hard whisper plants unforgettable tales in my deep memory.

The Son of Winter

The very faint bird doesn't shiver because of love or coldness. He just shakes his feather enjoying the winter's stories. Here, winter dresses a different color and a different cruelty and all that can I see are these pale shadows. Here, winter isn't tenderhearted; it is my grandfather's gloomy field where the bean swings over its grass as a sad bride. I am the son of winter; my ancestry had left me alone in this frosted lake. Look at my face; it is colorless; feel my hands; they are short and dead.

A Blind Winter

The pain is deep in winter, and the smiles have left our garden without goodbye. In its nights I am just a shadow over cold trees and in its days, I am a blind owl. This winter is blind and dry, nothing here but cold smiles and white dead flowers. Believe me, I have tried to plant a pink rose but the hands of this blind winter freeze my heart. Its gray mantle knows the roads of my mute lip and the coolness of my faceless moon.

Anwar Gheni Jaber is an Iraqi poet, writer and artist. He was born in 1973 in Babylon. His name has appeared in many literary magazines and anthologies and he has won many prizes; one of them is the "World Laureate-Best Poet in 2017 from WNWU". Tessellated (poems in one poem) narrative lyric writing and digital expressionistic art are his peculiar styles. Anwar is the author of "Narratopoet"; (2017), "Tessellation"; (2018) and other 60 books. His websites:

https://anwarjaber.wordpress.com

Amazon: https://amazon.com/author/anwarjaber

Little-Known Facts About the Great Philosophers

By Daniel Senser

Socrates got lost on the way to deliver
his Master's thesis, and lost every page
in a stiff wind. He didn't bother rewriting it.

Plato asked Socrates where the best place
to buy a gyro was. Plato
didn't include this in the Dialogues.

Diogenes lost his temper once.
He defended himself by saying
he didn't need it.

When asked to explain his concept
of the Ubermensch,
Nietchze stripped naked and
stood on the table, arms akimbo, saying:
"Observe, gentlemen!"

Kierkegaard once snatched a portrait
being drawn of him unsolicited
by an artist, crumpled it up,
put it in his mouth, and swallowed it.
"That will teach you to draw
a great man poorly!" he said.

A fly flew onto a piece of pecan pie
that Thomas Aquinas was eating.
When asked why he did not swat
the fly away, Aquinas said:
"The meek shall inherit the Earth,
and I want to be on their good side."

Foucault passed a group of children
playing in a park one day and smiled.
Then later he scolded himself for
taking the suppressive system of
socialization lightly.

Daniel Senser has been writing for about twelve years, primarily as a poet. Works of his have appeared in California Quarterly, Poetry Quarterly, Haiku Journal, and Jewish Currents, among other journals. he published a book of poetry about two and a half years ago entitled, "Chasing Crows." He graduated from the University of Cincinnati with a BA in English in 2014.

Nor Melt Away

By Fred Pollack

1

If I had lived a few more years
(and why shouldn't I have? Good genes,
hale satisfied centenarian),
I might have asked the following:
What is time but style?
In my youth, I wore the black uniform.
Some girls found it sexy, some scary,
which gave us a good way of judging girls.
(Men in black, it's well known, are serious.)
At his trial, Fat Hermann
said that in fifty years
there would be small statues of him
in every German home – very small, perhaps,
but there. He was decades off,
and might he have been visualizing bobbleheads?
Still … Then Grass, the novelist,
briefly a comrade, had someone
sing at the end (no doubt trying
to surrender to the Americans),

The trend is toward the bourgeois-smug.
For me it was. Without regret,
I abandoned stern nihilism
for the jaunty relativism
of commerce. Holidayed on nude beaches,
accepted my decadent children
and perverse grandchildren, even developed
some taste, as you can tell. But youth returns.

2

Griffin, archaeologist of the Anthropocene,
masked in the heat against hantavirus,
armed, exploring trailers and lean-tos
far from towns
in southeastern California and western Nevada,
found among the drifts and piles
a bundle of letters. The rubber-band
broke on touch. Neat penciled cursive,
school paper. Examinations
of feeling, immediate, honest, untainted
by literature, detailed
concern for mostly implied unspecified
problems, heartfelt considerate
advice, and hope (not, interestingly, faith)
continually urged … Nearby,
amidst receipts, bills,
tissues and droppings lay some polaroids
that had perhaps belonged. Green T-shirt,
blue dress, great hanging breasts and armflesh;

one of the faces puffy
from drink but neither visibly bruised.
Looking at them one imagined love
as high above the desert as any vulture.

3

If pain alone is real to us,
with violence as its faithful
sidekick and attorney, the old saw
"Life is a dream" has meaning.
Pain is the fuel of the dream,
whose work like that of poetry
is apotropaic: to deflect pain.
That inexplicable crowd
one day on Olympic or was it Pico
(new discount place?) was obviously dreaming.
Driving, whether on surface streets
or freeways, is a tense dream.
The position of any observer
is dreamlike. Shostakovich at the end
borrowed the xylophone from Saint-Saens's
"Skeleton Dance" for his own bones,
Rossini for an echo of his snide
youth. He believed the KGB
wouldn't get him now, something else would;
surveillance had been handed off.
"Good people on both sides"
at Nazi demonstrations
dream each other: as pain;

as opportunities for violence.
The important thing is not to use
the word "we" imprecisely,
certainly not for humanity at large.
"We" in the present case is Santa Monica.
When I was sick I went to a hospital.
I brought my notebook and three books
from the NYRB Classics series,
read, sweated, tried to read.
They found me a bed. I lay reading,
waiting for the specialist. And then I woke up.

4

An early-morning light-angle
where a ceiling meets a wall
resembles engineered effects
in shots of more expensive houses.
She has to go to the doctor.
He'll take her, and wait, though it's unnecessary
(next week she'll return the favor).
Then they'll shop, at an overpriced chain
that has outlived its reputation,
but its fruits remain good and they want fruit.
Returning, he'll do laundry
and attack the kitchen floor
with a Swiffer. (Even to mention
the maid who comes bi-weekly could
suggest discomfort that they have a maid
and ruin the delicate effect.)
Then while she cooks he'll take his evening pills

and feed the cat, who is already
leaping onto and off
the ledge beneath the ledge that holds her treats,
not sure that after a lifetime he'll remember.
(It may be sentimental to use the cat.)
With dinner, news, as much as bearable,
silenced when Trump appears
("That man doesn't speak in our house,"
she decreed and he approves),
unless the latest crime has been exceptional.
Later he asks what she's thinking.
She's thinking about the problems of a friend;
he, recalling an old article
decrying the tendency of mainstream poems
to end with bursts of vague philosophy.

Frederick Pollack - Author of two book-length narrative poems, *The Adventure* (Story Line Press, 1986) and *Happiness* (Story Line Press, 1998), and two collections, *A Poverty of Words* (Prolific Press, 2015) and *Landscape with Mutant* (Smokestack Books, 2018). In print, Pollack's work has appeared in Hudson Review, Southern Review, Salmagundi, Poetry Salzburg Review, Manhattan Review, Skidrow Penthouse, Main Street Rag, Miramar, Chicago Quarterly Review, The Fish Anthology (Ireland), Poetry Quarterly Review, Magma (UK), Neon (UK), Orbis (UK), and elsewhere. Online, his poems have appeared in Big Bridge, Diagram, BlazeVox, Mudlark, Occupoetry, Faircloth Review, Triggerfish, and elsewhere. Adjunct professor of creative writing at George Washington University.

A How For A Why

By John Garmon

I have been thinking lately that I wish I had a banjo.
I believe banjo players are happier than
people who play guitars.
The saddest of all the people in this country or another are
Those who do not play any kind of instrument.
Sometimes they sit at the side of the road weeping.
It is not their fault. The same goes for playing
The bass drum or the kettle drum or bongo drums or
The homemade drum with an untreated cowhide cover.
Music has too much percussion.
Once when I was in the outskirts of Medicine Hat,
I heard a man playing
What sounded like a sea captain's drum, like some kind of
Wood struck by a hard oak club. It had s hollow sound
Like a rock falling from a cliff on to an upside down canoe.
Bears came out of the forest to see what the sound was.
At first, they thought it was a woodpecker bouncing his
Brains against a pine tree infested by some insects
Similar to termites. The forest rang with loud drumbeats.
Squirrels scurried out on branches and looked down to see.

There was no need of a banjo, but there were no eagles
Perched at the topmost branches of the highest trees.
I remember hearing bells in the distance echoing. Yes.
It is possible for bells to echo. Anything bronze
Gives up a sound of village bells in Bavaria or Utah.
Banjos are instruments more people neglect and
Do not feel obligated to play. In Wyoming once
I drove over the Bighorn Mountains during a snowstorm.
It was in the middle of the night and I was lucky
I couldn't see how far my car would fall if I lost
Control and just let go when I went into a skid. The
Folks in Beatrice Nebraska have a few banjos. It
Isn't something they brag about, but they are proud
To be counted as an up and coming community.
When you ask them how they do it, they answer
Why does it matter? It is fun and it keeps us busy,
This way we are not liable to get into any trouble.

John Garmon was born in Texas in 1940. He earned a Ph.D. at Ball State University. His poetry has been in many magazines and books. He is a writing assistant at the College of Southern Nevada. He once served as president of Berkeley City College in California.

After Rain

By John Ronan

In the park, after rain, worms
Up for air crawl
Across asphalt walks
Unlike shadowless soil:
Sharp stone and sunlight,
Elbow room to the sky,
Early birds circling
And a single, smart-ass
Cloud shaped like bait.

What thoughts burden the worm?
Given a strict limit
Of three hundred neurons,
Inklings only: unease
At bitumen and drying winds,
Dimmest images of organ
Eyes or elbows, evolution
Gilding the siren dark.

Strollers step around the worms
For the most part, save
Some with a foot-flick
Back to the grass, squish
A few others, of course,
Putting them out of their misery,
Slight as that would seem to be.

John J. Ronan is a poet, playwright, movie/TV producer, and journalist. He has received national honors for his poetry and is a former NEA Fellow, Ucross Fellow, Bread Loaf Scholar, and Poet Laureate in Gloucester, MA, where his cable program The Writer's Block with John Ronan is beginning its 29th year. Poems have appeared in *Three Penny Review, New England Review, Southern Poetry Review, New York Quarterly, Folio,* and many other publications. Media productions have won a Telly, an Aurora Gold, a First for Education Programming from the NECTA, and have been aired on PBS outlets. In 2010 his book of poetry, Marrowbone Lane, was named a Highly Recommended selection by the Boston Authors Club. A new volume, *Taking the Train of Singularity South from Midtown,* appeared in January 2017. One of the poems from that book, "Good Harbor, Home," was set to music by the composer Rob Bradshaw; it premiered with the Salem Philharmonic in February, 2018. (TheRonan.org)

Blaze Pascal And The Courage Of Being (1)

By Kenneth Stephens

Once an old soul
lived in Contemplation,

a satellite city of the City of Angels near
the desert and the mountains and the sea.

From his cottage small and spare
he lifted his eyes to the hills
and saw Mount Contemplation,

which rose to the north in
the San Gabriel Range, his

humble abode set among
oak and jacaranda trees,
bougainvillaea and cedars,

myrtles and mesquite to the east,
pines and palms to the west,
watered by mountain streams.

His days were made pleasant
by mocking birds, bluejays,
robins, falcons, towhees,
eagles, and hummingbirds.

Daily he walked to the village and the
university, and up to the seminary
and the Garden of Ancient Trees,

where deep-toned chimes wafted on
ocean breezes from verandahs nearby.

The thin man wrote verses
every day and would say

things like, All flesh is grass,
and how life flies by at
downhill skateboard speed.

Why only yesterday
I was but a boy in
missionary boarding schools
in the Himalayas.

His speculations about being itself
rose from his own experience of life,

how the powers and particles
seek higher and higher ground,
yes, higher and higher ground,
against the waters of nonbeing,

how sapphires and fiery suns,
pale moons and diamond rings,

ballooning through space,
clustering and colliding,

are epiphanies all of
the courage of being.

And how in a billion light years the
powers and particles by secret strife

give birth to life and
the fight for freedom,
freedom from fear,

freedom from a life
with no meaning,
with no love or
opportunity to
learn and create.

Kenneth D. Stephens is originally from India, where he attended Christian missionary boarding schools in the Himalayas. He came to the United States to go to theological seminary, after which he went on to do his Ph.D in philosophy. His memoir The Meaning of These Days: Memoir of a Philosophical Pastor was published by Wipf and Stock. He is an active member of the African Wildlife Foundation, the Wilderness Society, and other environmental organizations, and resides on the outskirts of Los Angeles County.

Amulet - voice of Penelope

By Mary Jane White

62

All the young men came in
But you were never there
Standing as likely under a rafter
Off-center
Visible enough

63

As a still small-footed
Never old & wandering vine
Your trunk the exact imperfect
Square pillar

64

Light red leaves
On a low breeze lifted
Disobediently

65

A silver-tongued solitary of the moon
& of the oxygen atom

66

So I felt the urge to run & listen for you
Here where the breeze compresses the blossom
Raises the stems

67

I heard you
Your instep
Swivel & lift

68

An open sky
Upon every tread as you turned
So then I hesitated to listen
& the breezes stopped hiding you
So busy
Reflective of dark silence
Alertness & execution
So before I heard anything given or taken
I believed I knew your beastly mind

69

Bloodied all those young men
Felled in close quarters
Their alarms & piercing cries
As they departed
Who were they
The worthless

70

Even our frontiers were murmuring that moment
Who were they

71

& I sat
Answering myself
Marrying the unseen with my own answer

72

Satiated
How am I thus satiated
When I have never since eaten
Nor opened my hand
Nor opened my eye
Nor opened my belly nor my heart
Nor unstopped my ears

Nor disarranged myself
In the least

73

All this effort is useless
To break my coldness with blunt percussions
I no longer require axe heads
But crave sweetness

74

Restrain myself as I must
Of necessity
My ear at my door
May I avoid drowning in these tears & gasping
As the fresh salt breezes press in

75

Blood holds half the sky in its arc
& from my rooms
I listen carelessly
Since I am one with you
Who disregard mercy

76

Listen under your rafter
As we close on cruelty

& I know how all will resume
With me after this
Your familiar novelty
Your low tone loosened

77

& it is out of my mind
I must listen for what is inhuman
Out of my mind must hear
What the low tree-line against the horizon conceals

78

That sea that ever disturbs your busy heart
Since I have already listened long
For you among younger men
Even as the sinking fog departed with you

79

Not for the first time I laugh quietly to myself
Dear man
What are you doing
Stacking coins or cards to pass time
You with a pastime

80

Or am I never
To gauge

Your character
For all it is
Or what passes
As we lie
Listless in winter
My hands fallen
To my sides
Helpless
To circumstance

81

I will not be visible but will make no retreat
An amulet in your pocket

82

I will lie as I have lain
In our house
Waiting & tried

83

Again satiated
May I drink deeply
Of pomegranate
Swallow the dregs of it
May I wipe its stain
Scour granite

84

Stream running to the sea
Sky in it below the tree-root
& sea breezes rising
Then may I hardly be there
As the morning has gone & returned
 & is scattered widely
With half the house
& its furnishings

85

Then may I throw all our corpses out
Walk in the salty air
As you my consort
Lead me for the moment through town
Secure in your honored anonymity
& feared in the streets their fathers also walk
Where our new passion withers
Withers while everybody watches
Sports foot races or martial contests
Where I also come to lose myself
& can drop everything watching
Our open-hearted boy my joy
In his tamer pursuits

86

Where I can run in place
Or raise the alarm of the newest cacophony
Even that fading away of all youth
That is this very instant screaming
A shrill blare we may never know here
Since no one in particular of any stature
Is sounding it

87

Since I can't lose
My head now
Or in the sunlight
Lose you
My nearest & ancient hope

Mary Jane White, MFA Iowa Writers' Workshop, NEA Fellowships (in poetry and translation). Tsvetaeva translations: *Starry Sky to Starry Sky* (1988) *New Year's, an elegy for Rilke* (Adastra Press, 2007); *Poem of the Hill* (The New England Review); *Poem of the End* (The Hudson Review), reprinted in Poets Translate Poets, (Syracuse 2013).

Fragments Washed Ashore

By Richard Weaver

The sky is shrouded in mystery tonight.
The stars undone.

A green dragon hawk chases
a blue dragon hawk across the lagoon.
Will they mate to the gulfs' delight
or the gulls'?

I watch a hummingbird frozen in thistle.
The sun argues like cheap wine.

The first wind this evening
races like fire along the beach.
I stand basking in its path.

Caught in the undertow
man is returned to face trial
and sentenced to life on land.

The birds come here because they must.
Take flight all who can.

On the island politics are kept
in their place: the alligators pretend
their rule is absolute
while the birds perch where they please.

Over me the man o'wars circling the sun.
Their shadows fall, lifeless
into the open arms of the gulf.

A frantic mother.
Another empty nest.
Not even a cottonmouth in residence.
Surely the wind must be stealing
the pale blue eggs.

Something between wind and rain,
somewhere beneath the oyster's reluctance
to leave its bed,
sometimes in the narrow light
that escapes the stars,
somehow in the morning song
of the hermit thrush,
all that I seek.

On the way I saw a world afire,
turned and caught

out of the corner of one eye
a heron spinning in the air,
as if fire and air were twins.
and water and earth orphans.

Richard Weaver lives in Baltimore's Inner Harbor where he volunteers at the Maryland Book Bank, and acts as the Archivist-at-large for a Jesuit College founded in 1830. He also acts as a seasonal snow-flake counter, unofficially. Recent poems from this MS have appeared in 2River View, Gingerbread House, Clade Song, Conjunctions (web), Aberration Labyrinth, & Twisted Vine Leaves.

Because of Everything

By Sandra Kolankiewicz

I had less time than I thought but finished any
        way, what husbands would call passive

aggressive in my desire to complete
        what I have begun even if I don't

like the end I see coming. While some won't
        start, and others cannot stop, I'm compelled

to do both, even following through on
        what I don't believe in, the DNA

involved probably the biggest reason my
        line dies out with me after surviving

for no reason through the previous and
        innumerable generations. All

ends here with cats scratching even after
        the flea medicine's applied, dog looking

over his shoulder as if I have done
        something unforgivable by having

managed to collect rooms full of things that
        would disappear under dust but for being

swept spotless by the woman who has come
        to clean every Tuesday for thirty years.

Sandra Kolankiewicz's poems have been accepted by London Magazine, New World Writing, Into the Void, Crannog, BlazeVox, Gargoyle, Prairie Schooner, Fifth Wednesday, and Per Contra. *Turning Inside Out* was released by Black Lawrence Press. Finishing Line Press has published *The Way You Will Go* and *Lost in Transition*. *When I Fell*, a novel with 76 color illustrations, is available at Web-e-Books.

A Secret

By Marc Carver

We are all fools
wandering around
doing things for no real reason
crashing off each other like snooker balls
hoping one day we may do something of brilliance
so everybody can say how great we are
only to realize
how unimportant it is to be recognised by others
even of greatness.
But on we go
trying to grasp onto that passing cloud
looking for something
trying to find something
but the secret is
it is never quite what we thought it to be.

Marc Carver has been a writer a long time now and hope that he has given some pleasure to others and this is why he continues to write.

Leave It All on the Field

By Michelle Brooks

A man less than a mile from my house
has shut down the highway. He's standing
on the bridge over which I drive almost
every day, and he's threatening to jump.
He won't despite people yelling, Just
jump already and *Kill yourself.* The police
close the road that leads to him, fearing
the shouts will push him over the edge.
This won't end until almost midnight.

I watch the Super Bowl, staring at the semi-
trucks and cars that have been diverted. They
creep past as I eat a bowl of French Onion dip.
The Eagles win, and fans trash the city, so great
their happiness. I'd like to say I don't understand
any of this, that I don't know what it's like to feel
too much or not enough. That I'd never stuffed pain
so deep that it both rots and explodes. I'd like to say
that things like this don't happen in my neighborhood.

Michelle Brooks has published a collection of poetry, *Make Yourself Small*, (Backwaters Press), and a novella, *Dead Girl, Live Boy*, (Storylandia Press). Her poetry collection, *Flamethrower*, will be published by Latte Press in 2019. A native Texan, she has spent much of her adult life in Detroit.

What To Wear?

By Greg J. Moglia Jr.

White shirt, striped tie, black slacks
and the grey tweed sports jacket
always that tweed sport jacket
while for years the Vietnam war and there I was

My surface the same - no protest in me
only the daily watch and read…the daily upset inside
Years and thousands dead and still there I am in tweed
Teaching Physics to high schoolers

In Hitler's Germany as he took away the thousands
in all the towns the bakers still baked
How they felt I do not know but
on the surface I am there with them

What in hell should I have done?
Keep to baking as neighbors disappear?
Or throw down my sport jacket
 do more than bear witness?

Entrapped and to my heart
was I a hold for the faults?
Left to dare children to imagine
an open - ended world

Greg Moglia is a veteran of 27 years as Adjunct Professor of Philosophy of Education at N.Y.U and 37 years as a high school teacher of Physics and Psychology. His poems have been accepted in over 300 journals in the U.S., Canada, England, India, Australia, Sweden and Austria as well as five anthologies. He is 8 times a winner of an ALLEN GINSBERG Poetry Award sponsored by the poetry center at Passaic County Community College. He lives in Huntington, N.Y.

A Zephyr

By Souzi Gharib

{In memory of my father}

A zephyr so full of zeal and zest
invigorated my tender wings,
he made my flights with soaring blest
my songs so resonant with vibrancy.

A wakeful eye
refusing sleep
when an ailing child befriended bed,
a fever-cooling lullaby would seep
into the scorching sands of head.

An ear that loved the vesper bell,
the chanting of monastic birds,
adored the choruses of frogs which well
in the heart of night with mooing herds.

A verdant hand that tended flowers,
that nursed a wounded bird of prey,

so Marsha, the falcon who glowers,
becomes his mate,
a friend to stay.

A man partial to the blue attire,
a glowing blue-bell's
or the sky's,
an elegance that was never to tire
of pilot-shirts
or navy ties.

A voluble pen
a warbling stream
exposing ills
unmasking wrongs
an utterance that was found extreme,
if extreme are rectifying songs.

Susie Gharib is a graduate of the University of Strathclyde (Glasgow, Scotland) with a Ph.D. Her doctoral thesis, entitled Stylistic and Thematic Reassessment of The Trespasser, is a critical study of the work of D.H. Lawrence. Since 1996, she has been lecturing in Syria. She self-published four collections of poetry (My Love in Red, The Alpine Glow, Resonate and Kareem) and a collection of short stories (Bare Blades). She is a lover of Nature and enjoys swimming.

The Power Of The Impossible

By Jeton Kelmendi

Only forward in the barely naked road
Ampleness is twice to stop her walk,
Do not stand by.
—Tomas Tranströmer, Nobel Prize 2011

Surprisingly
How far is this close.

It can't be seen even when eyes
Are descending one after another;
Spirits are connected
Even when thoughts are not met.

I am able to help myself
Stay this close, you are looking at me,
I know, you are forgetting, completely
You are ignoring me.

I pray for the tradition of the possible
The impossible of the impotent.

Dreams and desires for another meaning
Are spread in one hundred options,
While your mind is imagining
Impossible elements are taking power.

Two names,
Connect with two words.

You must return inside yourself,
Even the impossible has its own,
Options,
They come and go
Two different things:
The reason and the lack of reason,
And I return inside myself
You are more powerful in the impossible
Emigration;

I want to escape from myself
Until it comes with me,
It departs sometimes:
Sometime it arrives
A possibility, of evil
In every religion;
A material, just like all bodies together
In the sky
It was grown,
It will remain small
In front of the love that I have

For you, for myself
And become convinced,
Trust the possibilities, or even yourself
What must be said better?

In the middle of your forehead
Hit your head,
Escape from yourself,
From the impossible;
Scream your words
Your thoughts
Since they are yours,
I promise you twice
For me and for you;

Today becomes tomorrow,
Yesterday becomes today,
Do not delay our journey
The truth is becoming a dream.

Jeton Kelmendi - Poet, player, publicist, translator, publisher and a professor of university and academic. Born in the city of Peja, Kosovo, in 1978, he completed elementary school in his birth place. Later he continued his studies at the University of Pristina and received the degree of Bachelor of Arts in Mass communication. He completed his graduate studies at the Free University of Brussels, Belgium, specializing in International and Security Studies. He finished his second master degree in diplomacy. Kelmendi did a PhD in the "Influence of media in EU Political Security Issues". He is professor at AAB University College. He is active member of the European Academy of Science and Arts in Salzburg Austria. For many years he has written poetry, prose, essays and short stories. He is a regular contributor to many newspapers, in Albania and abroad, writing on many cultural and political topics, especially concerning international affairs. Jeton Kelmendi became well known in Kosova, after the publication of his first book entitled: "The Century of Promises" ("Shekulli i Premtimeve"), published in 1999. Later he published a number of other books. His poems were translated in more that twenty-seven languages and published in several international Literature Anthologies. He is the most translated Albanian Poet and well known in Europe. According to a number of literary critics, Kelmendi is the genuine representative of modern Albanian poetry. International critics and poets wrote for him a lot of article, considering him as great European poet. He is a member of many international poetry clubs and is a contributor to many literary and cultural magazines, especially in English, French and Romanian Languages. The wisdom of his work in the field of Literature is based in the attention that he pays to the poetic expression, modern exploration of the text and the depth of the message. His Genre is focused more on love lyrics and elliptical verse intertwined with metaphors and artistic symbolism. Currently resides and works in Brussels, Belgium and in Pristina, Kosovo.

Shooting Star

By Shari Jo LeKane

Upon the early fall of night
my eyes behold a shooting star,
electric streak in twilight sea,
now here alive, then gone you are.

What beauty brings this lustrous light
well driven by some cosmic czar
whose alien powers surely be
from planets we believe afar?

To capture such a fleeting sight
and save it in a mason jar
so that it could not ever flee
and hold my wish in reservoir!

Oh, incandescent beam so bright
who burns amidst the midnight mar
and disappears without a plea
then leaves no single star on par.

Shari Jo LeKane (B.A. English, Spanish; M.A. Spanish - Saint Louis University Madrid/St. Louis) lives in St. Louis, Missouri, writes articles, literary critiques, poetry and prose. She is a consultant for not-for-profit, business, community development, education, leadership development, disability, and elderly advocacy, and she teaches Spanish Language and Culture in a local university, and creative writing to men in a maximum-security jail and to special needs students. She wrote a novel in verse, Poem to Follow, two books of poetry, Fall Tenderly and Surviving Gracefully, and is featured in several poetry anthologies, including the Missouri VSA 2013 Anthology, Turning the Clocks Forward Again; Poetica Victorian; Red Dashboard Disorder Anthology: Mental Illness and Its Effects; Think Pink; The Muse India/Createspace Anthology Of Present Day Best Poems (Vols. I, II, III & IV); Bordertown Press Poetry of People on the Move; The Society of Classical Poets (Vol. I, VI); The Mas Tequila Review; Snapping Twig; The Lonely Crowd; Form Quarterly; Devolution Z; The Quarterday Review; Adelaide Literary Magazine; Adelaide Literary Awards Poetry Finalist Best of 2017 Anthology; Adelaide Voices Literary Award for Poetry Shortlist Winner for 2018; MacroMicroCosm Literary and Arts Review: Solstice; The Road Not Taken; The Faircloth Review; Bindweed; Halcyon Days; Lunaris Review; Iconoclast; The Poeming Pigeon; Unrequited: An Anthology of Love Poems about Inanimate Objects; and Literature Today International Journal of Contemporary Literature (Vols. I, II, & VI). Shari's poetry has been published in several literary magazines in the U.S., Canada, England, India, Ireland, Nigeria, Portugal, Scotland, Spain and Wales, and she has been featured in spoken word on the award-winning CD, 'How Live?' with LOOPRAT. Shari considers herself a modern formalist, addressing contemporary issues in poetic verse with a stylized language.

To The Fullest

By Georgia Eugenides

we forget the umbrella in the car on purpose
we say "this is what it feels like to be alive"
we zigzag across the city, absorb the drizzle,
sway in the September gloom like
seaweed soaking up sun

head-on collision while we're waiting
for the light to turn green;
laced fingers jerk apart

windshield shatters and reminds me of
my mother's creole vase
knocked over in the living room
(both were accidents)

Sirens sound from cop cars, lure
nosy neighbors instead of Odysseus,
driver bathes in regretful-red &
thinks of all the "i love you's" he never said

we buy a see-through poncho
from a vendor down the street
shakily discard a Twenty

Georgia Eugenides is an eighteen-year-old poet who grew up in Berlin, Germany; Chicago, IL and Princeton, NJ. Her first poem was published when she was nine years old. She spent the previous summer interning at The Paris Review.

Walking

By Patrick Hurley

(selection)

22.05
dark reflections calm
amidst sharp angles

numbers and names
assigned to straight lines

hidden in an optical fold
is a blue conveyance

a reminder of
other directions
a remainder of
other orientations

smell of gasoline floods
this chipped-paint landscape

two new poles
have been erected—

are these to do with
some ritual
some mystery?

or are they part of
the scaffolding of commerce?

on the calligrapher's finger
an ink smudge—any shape
might suggest signification

the paranoiac raves
in a matrix of
invented categories

the filmstrip has
been run too
many times

reality is now
faded and scratched

Patrick Hurley taught writing and literature at various colleges for almost 20 years. Now he makes poems (and tends bar to pay the bills). His work has appeared multiple times in The Adelaide Literary Review (where he was the top finalist for the 2017 Poetry Award and Adelaide Voices Literary Award for Poetry Finalist for 2018), The Alchemist Review, Clockwise Cat, Futures Trading, Eunoia, and The Furious Gazelle. He has poems upcoming in Poetry Pacific, The Quail Bell Magazine, Be Untexed, and Ground Fresh Thursday. For years he has been working on a long poetry project called walking. It will be finished this summer.

The One Behind The All

By Monica Timbal

I see the world through million eyes,
Those suffering souls, these aching hearts
Mellow, carefree children's laughter
Are all my own.
Those leaning trees, feel them sway
Look! flying birds and falling rain
Running beasts, rushing streams, ocean waves-
My very face.
In all the places
Through all the eyes
I am the eternal seer.
I am the oversoul,
I am the One behind the many,
I am the One behind the all.

Monica Timbal is in the process of publishing her first spiritual poetry book "Butterfly Flutters", and is completing her second book. Her poetry comes out of life-long practice of yoga and meditation, and a vision that penetrates beyond what is merely visible to the naked eye. This vision is of a transcendental oneness underlying reality. Her poetry aims at giving the reader glimpses into this perspective, through the ephemeral nature of life.

Returning To The Table

By Laura Solomon

After some time I return to the table.
I check the corridor in both directions
To see if it is safe.

Are my myriad enemies, my detractors,
Hiding behind chairs,
Ready to spring out and lacerate me for fun?

It's like shooting bullets at a ghost.

Here I come, down the main corridor
Like the marshmallow man in Ghostbusters
Destroying buildings and roads,
My footsteps leave no trace on the floor.

Only dust in my wake.

I hear echoes from further down the hall;
The coast's clear. Come on out. Come on out and have fun.
Don't let the bastards grind you to nothing,

Forget about what they done –
Here it is, your space at your table,
The chair pulled out waiting for you to take a seat.

My leaden limbs fall foot after heavy foot upon the floor.
My face is paralysed; my tongue frozen in my head.
What the hell am I going to say?

I sit and wait for the word, an angel at this table,
The page remains as blank as snow, you know,
What the hell am I going to…
I pick up the pen and make a dark red mark, an X.

It's all I have to say to you,
The one who will come after,
The 'yes' after the 'no',
Cover your hair and your eyes,
Drive on through the darkness,
Drive on through the night,
Stay long enough in the blackness,
And the dark will turn to light.

Laura Solomon has a 2.1 in English Literature (Victoria University, 1997) and a Masters degree in Computer Science (University of London, 2003).

Her books include Black Light, Nothing Lasting, Alternative Medicine, An Imitation of Life, Instant Messages, Vera

Magpie, Hilary and David, In Vitro, The Shingle Bar Sea Monster and Other Stories, University Days, Freda Kahlo's Cry, Brain Graft, Taking Wainui, Marsha's Deal and Hell's Unveiling.

She has been short-listed in Bridport, Edwin Morgan, Ware Poets, Willesden Herald, Mere Literary Festival, and Essex Poetry Festival competitions.

She was short-listed for the 2009 Virginia Prize and the 2014 International Rubery Award and won the 2009 Proverse Prize. She has had work accepted in the Edinburgh Review, Orbis and Wasafiri (UK), Takahe and Landfall (NZ). She has judged the Sentinel Quarterly Short Story Competition.

Her play 'The Dummy Bride' was part of the 1996 Wellington Fringe Festival and her play 'Sprout' was part of the 2005 Edinburgh Fringe Festival.

At Père Lachaise

By Byron Beynon

Here the famous guests are scattered
in funerary plots and calculated divisions,
with sculpture, some reminding me of sentry-boxes,
ready and made to accommodate whole families.
During the hour or more
I stayed among the dead
I found the black and polished grave of Proust,
his name remembered in time and letters.
I searched for Balzac, Bizet,
and the young American
Jim Morrison of the Doors.
Blind men! But who's to say?
One by one the shadows disappeared.
At 89e Div 1-2 I saw
graffiti on Epstein's monument
to Oscar Wilde,
Oscar who? Someone had scrawled
in dark paint.
A gardener pointed
to Piaf's place,

smothered in flowers and notes,
as children from a school party
sketched Chopin's marble face.
Nobody could disturb them,
they had completed their cycle
in a city touched by sunshine and dust,
where unknown visitors leave bouquets,
vulnerable petals that see in the light.

Byron Beynon lives in Wales. His work has appeared in several publications including San Pedro River Review, Agenda, Quadrant, Poetry Pacific, London Magazine and the human rights anthology In Protest (University of London and Keats House Poets). Collections include Cuffs (Rack Press), Human Shores (Lapwing Publications) and The Echoing Coastline (Agenda Editions).

Forecast

By Marc Frazier

*Listen, whatever it is you try / to do with your life /
nothing will ever dazzle you / like the dreams of your body*
— Mary Oliver

Dreams flare like flamingos into more light.
Somewhere over blue fields is the form my spirit will go to
when the dreams of my body   have lived their separate lives.
Each star begins apart from itself.
Each moment is lost.
The sum of us is ponderable.
The dreamer, not the dream, is impossible.
I know your solid hands around me in the
blue shadows of this tropical dusk.
I will never set down all that I carry.
But I feel I will when we balance the
moon on a hurricane-strewn limb.
I am through considering ways for my body to revolt.
I am through with the debris of love.
With boarding up windows.
Escape routes.

I will swim into surf until it or my body tires.
Choose the strongest words upon
which to build my thoughts.
Dispose of the weak loves of my past lives.
Split the atom with my resolve.
Want within reason.
Bear the unbearable into the eye's calm.
Rest and grow stronger until I have no choice.
I pray for each gull without favor.
Build a sturdy life from what is left.

Marc Frazier has poetry in journals including *The Spoon River Poetry Review, ACM, Good Men Project, f(r)iction, The Gay and Lesbian Review, Slant, Permafrost, Plainsongs,* and *Poet Lore* and excerpts from his memoir WITHOUT in *Gravel, The Good Men Project, decomP, Autre, Cobalt, Evening Street Review, and Punctuate.* Marc, an LGBTQ+ writer, is the recipient of an Illinois Arts Council Award for poetry and has been nominated for a Pushcart Prize. His book *The Way Here* and two chapbooks are available on Amazon as well as his second full-length collection Each Thing Touches (Glass Lyre Press). His website is www.marcfrazier.org.

The Drifters

By John Sweeder

Mid-autumn mornings just after a fierce
coastal storm, I walk along a quiet beach
scavenging for pitted shards of sea-glass
with their frosted greens and ambers;
for sea-shells, those exoskeletons of scallops
and clams; for curvilinear whelk
egg cases—Nature's Slinkys.

I overturn a horseshoe crab and finger
a black shark's tooth. I hoist an ashen conch
shell to my ear and listen for the sound
of the crashing ocean surf. I spot pieces
of gray weathered pine and wonder whether
they have wandered from a boat dock
or washed up from under the boardwalk.

I pursue these peripatetic ocean remnants
to remind myself of my sandy childhood treks
along the more crowded summer beach
where, amid the drifting sounds of carousels

and roller coasters, and smells of crab cakes
and curly fries, my nature walks came and went
more quickly than I had wished they had.

John Sweeder is a retired professor from La Salle University in Philadelphia, PA. A poet and memoirist, he has had his work published in Adelaide Literary Magazine, Burningword Literary Journal, Shantih, Haiku Journal, River Poets Journal, Ancient Paths Online, and The Opening Line Literary 'Zine, among other venues. A Finalist of the Adelaide Literary Award for Poetry 2018, John is listed in Poets & Writers Directory of Poet & Writers; has completed his first chapbook entitled, Wonderwheel Dreams & Nightmares: 26 poems to Charm and Alarm; and has self-published Breathing through a Straw: A Memoir for Baby Boomers and Neurotic Catholics at https://jsweeder.wordpress.com/ as well as Faith Genes for the Blue Jean Generation: A Self-help Memoir at

https://www.amazon.com/Faith-Genes-Blue-Jean-Genera-tion-ebook/dp/B07BH84DY1

Remembering Red

By Marc Simon

On Saturdays, when other Jews sat and stood in synagogues
My Uncle Red lay on his back
Under my father's jacked up 1958 Rambler American
In his dark blue work shirt with his name patch, "Red."
His given name was Nathan but whoever called him that,
I don't know.

He kept a plug of Mail Pouch in his cheek as he
Changed oil, torqued bolts, tightened belts, tweaked tie rods,
While my father and I handed him greasy tools
Or the juice jar, as he called it, so he could spit.
Red had big hands and big shoulders and anchors
Tattooed on the insides of his forearms,
Where unluckier Jews of his generation
had numbers tattooed on theirs.
He said he served in the Pacific. That's all he would say.

Summer camp for me was a weekend every July
At my Uncle Red's rough-hewn, cold-water camp he'd built
Mostly by himself in Emlenton, PA

In a clearing in the piney woods.
It wasn't like the summer camps some friends attended:
No color wars, swimming trophies, candy drops,
ghost stories, archery or sing-alongs
But with Red as my counselor,
I learned to bait a line and clean a trout and
make a fire and crap in the woods.

When we sat Shiva for my father Red sat with us, too,
Fidgeting in his blue serge suit and white shirt and tie,
Holding a Mason jar for his tobacco juice.
He sat and said nothing; what could he say,
He'd lost his little brother.
Before he left the room he stuck some
money into my mother's hand.
I followed him outside, and we stood
in the freezing March wind
And he asked me how I liked being a hotshot college boy,
And when was I going to come up to the camp to visit,
And I said soon, soon, soon as I can,
But of course with my term papers and
frat parties and protest marches
And committees and internships and requisite drugs,
I never did.

The last time I saw Red his hair was white.
The "Sugar"—that's what my mother called diabetes,
As if sweetening its name could diminish it effect—
Had taken his left leg, up to the hip.

He lived in the Hebrew Home, where poorer Pittsburgh Jews
Were warehoused if the family couldn't afford or didn't care
To spend the money on more gracious private care.
I'd brought along a pack of Mail Pouch,
for sentimental reasons,
Mostly my own, I guess.
Red through thick glasses recognized me
and called me Marky like he used to.
He asked about my father and why his
little brother never came to visit,
And I told him, well, Dad sends his
love, and I'm sure he had.
Then, for a little while, we talked about fishing.

Marc Simon's short fiction has appeared in several literary magazines, including The Wilderness House Review, Flashquake,Poetica Magazine, The Writing Disorder, Jewish Fiction.net,Slush Pile Magazine,Everyday Fiction, The Adelaide Literary Magazine and Burningword Literary Magazine. His debut novel, The Leap Year Boywas published in December, 2012. Marc lives in Naples, Florida.

A Model Of Bliss

By Boris Kokotov

He's built a railroad in the basement
of his house. A hundred yards
of shiny rails, numerous locomotives,
couches, terminals, waiting platforms,
bridges, tunnels, houses, and various figures:
travelers with luggage, schoolchildren
at a bus stop, a policeman, a couple
of dogs, a group of deer by a small pond.
The layout is carefully thought through:
stations distributed along the loops,
a couple of crossing shanties smartly sited,
tiny cameras fitted inside the coach,
the control panel set next to the entry steps,
a projector aimed at a big white screen
across the room, speakers scattered around,
bundles of wire hidden beneath the structure.
This is the ongoing project: routes being changed,
terminals replaced, dummies added.
He presses a few buttons and everything
springs to life: locomotives are moving,

signals blinking, engines hissing, cars honking,
dogs barking. Images appear on the screen:
passengers sitting quietly by the window
of a car, scenery floating outside.
Over the years it cost him a fortune.
While the rest of his house is neglected,
the world downstairs is neat as a new pin.
He used to invite a few guests — neighbors,
acquaintances, their kids, strangers —
for the show lasting half an hour.
Occasionally he mused about charging spectators
a modest fee, but he never did it.
He retired several years ago, when his wife
got sick with cancer. He promptly put in
a hospital with a chapel at crossroads
and began running an ambulance through
red lights with sirens on. After the battle
was lost, he installed a funeral home
and a cemetery at the foot of the hill.
He also planted some trees along the road.
Nowadays we rarely see him outside.
The lights in the windows are usually off,
which is not alarming; we know where
he is: downstairs, busy with trains.
Everything is running smoothly, everything
is under control. An express arrives, the crowd
spills out, fluent motion, restrained laughter...
The subtle workings of his model of bliss.

Boris Kokotov was born in Moscow, Russia. Currently he lives in Baltimore. He writes poems and short stories in both Russian and English languages. His translations from German Romantics were published in the anthology "Vek Perevoda" (The Century of Translation) in Moscow. His translation of Louise Glück's "The Wild Iris" was nominated for the best translation of the year 2012 in Russia.

Night Passengers

By Joseph Buehler

Banked against the sky:
perhaps invisible clouds piled high
somewhere overhead and below,
strategically placed lights in darkness,
water, the Gulf, barely discernible houses.
This moment should be captured---it is
not to be relinquished. Yet it will not
last eternally; its nature is ephemeral.

Blackness can be your friend, you know,
so don't cast it away from you---those
lights and that darkness down below are
now swiftly fading away in the wake
of the jetpath.

Joseph Buehler has published over 60 poems by the summer of 2017 in ArLiJo, Nine Mile Magazine, Sentinel Literary Quarterly in the U.K., Serving House Journal, Futures Trading, Green Hills Literary Lantern, Indiana Voice Journal and elsewhere. he is retired and lives in Georgia with his wife Trish.

Ineffable Of Life

By Abby Ripley

Where does the dancer begin
And the dance stop? How can
You be one without the other?
A paradox that Yeats wondered about.

Centuries before Heraclitus
Declared that you can't step
In the same river twice since
Change is everywhere in the world.

After that Plotinus drew attention
To the things that were
At once same but different
Or everything and nothing at all.

And now we have Mandelbrot fractals
That are mathematically generated
By using an output as an input
Like a chain link that turns on itself to move forward.

From there to feedback theory or cybernetics
To self-replication and onward in complexity
To transformations one into another
It is the ineffable of living studied dialectically today.

What is living but the opposite of dying
Dying the emergence of nothing
Nothing the emptiness of space and being
Being the presence of soul and hope

Hope: flat without imagination
Imagination is fecundity and creation
Creation is ground zero of life
Life is circularity and vision

Vision is foresight and hindsight
Hindsight is completion and wisdom
Wisdom is the "wise" in "dom"
Dumb is to exist in silence

Silence is the ceasing of noise
Noise is the interference in sound
Sound is the ear's music
Music is the sacrament of the universe

Universe is simultaneously near and far
Far is out of sight
Sight is an eyeful of information
Information is smart form

Form and inform are inseparable
Inseparable and dependent give trust
Trust insures reliability
Reliability allows movement

Movement is the state of move and mover
Just as digging describes dig and digger
And dancing the magic of dance and dancer
All of these make life better but are not life.

I am a 75-year-old woman who was born and raised on a cattle ranch in the state of Montana, on the Crow Indian Reservation. I am not a Crow, but my paternal great grandmother was half Oglala Sioux. The ranch was on the reservation, not because of my father's heritage, rather for the reason that Indian land could be leased inexpensively, and his father-in-law, my grandfather, was one of the biggest ranchers in the area.

I attended the little Indian school, and there had my first creative writing experience. In the eighth grade I wrote a nature poem for the school newspaper. The principal of the school commented: "Who do we have here? Another Walt Whitman?" I did know Whitman since my teacher required that all eighth-graders memorize and recite one hundred poems by the end of the year. Whitman was included, and his free verse appealed to me then. It still appeals to me, and as a break from the historical novel I am writing, I've taken to penning poetry again. Appearing in this anthology is the first time I've been published as a poet, and I'm very excited about it.

I've spent most of my life as a student, but also as a Peace Corps volunteer, a travel agent, a life insurance field agent, an editor, a fine art photographer/exhibitor, a painter, and now a novelist/poet. I live with my partner of forty three years, three dogs, and a magical Calico cat in the countryside of Connecticut. I also crusade on behalf of African people who suffer from tungiasis, alerting humanitarian, political, and religious leaders to this scourge.

The Poet I Am

By Ralph Geeplay

I supposed I was a poet
whose ink was gilded
With rich entrée that
Was settled and intrepid.
I assumed I could bray the
Stony frothing ocean
And see the dolphin
Skate generously for free.
I thought myself a poet,
Hiking the sandy beach.
Then I stood doubted,
Nervous, a handout to bleach
The silver cobwebs divorcing
The seas from the cloud
Then watched Mona
Go by, wrapped in a shroud.

A poet, I held; I recognized
What happiness was—
Jazz and trumpets flowing

In a midafternoon cafe, jaws
Apart, in awe looking for novelty,
And solitude that delights.
Or waking early and seeing
Cracks pour light.
I was that poet, modest
In actions fivefold—

Then I misplaced my
Passions, apathetic, and cold.
A difficult man alright, alone
In his travelling mind.
Taking in the beauty, the
Ersatz, waltz, and confined.
The fear, of a poet who was
Supposed to be brave
Now vulnerable, torpid,
Puny, thirsty for a crave
To shake the hands of
Kipling, but and only, IF.*
He considers his travail,
Soup, alone in his enclave;
Right there, with ink link to paper.

I supposed I was a poet
Whose ink was golden
With rich bite and wit that
Was firm and fearless, am I?

IF* the author's favorite poem by R. Kipling

Ralph Cherbo Geeplay was born in Pleebo, Southeastern Liberia, West Africa. Geeplay published his first set of poems in 2009 in the Liberian Sea Breeze Journal, and edited by Stephanie Horton. A Pan African poet, he writes about Africa, the Liberian civil war, his Grebo heritage, and everything in between. He recently published his poetry in the Blue Lake Review, and the Adelaide Literary Magazine for which he a finalist. He is the editor of an online journal, The Liberian Listener, and lives in Edmonton Alberta, Canada, with his family.

Eurydice

By Chella Courington

Women have cried over my confinement
in hell by a husband who loved me so
he could not turn away
could not abide the caveat.
These long dark days
underground
breathless
I have not lived yearning for him.
I'm fine.

Did you really believe he wanted me
on earth with him?
Orpheus?
The beloved singer?
What would he sing if I were there?
For his song he needed me
buried beneath the crushing ground
star-crossed love that could never vanish
because it never was.
He didn't desire a woman

bloody with menstrual rituals
whose body once luminous would be taken by time.
Orpheus could not accept such a betrayal.
He wanted me as nymph, not crone.

Even more than age
he feared my voice.
Afraid it would rise above his.
What did he know of suffering and forgiveness?
I was the one severed from the sun
shut in subterranean darkness
barely enough oxygen.

He could have joined me the day I descended.
A knife to his throat, a serpent to his breast.
But he did none of these.
Came to me later by other hands.
I have no use for him.

Chella Courington is a writer and teacher. With a Ph.D. in American and British Literature and an MFA in Poetry, she is the author of six poetry and three flash fiction chapbooks. Her poetry appears in numerous anthologies and journals including Spillway, Gargoyle, Pirene's Fountain, and The Los Angeles Review. Originally from the Appalachian South (USA), Courington lives in California with another writer and two cats.

Untitled

By Matthew Nino Azcuy

She graces her letters
With a feminine ease
She is strong with color
A pink flashing;
A serene

She is walking perfection
The selection for me

She is cold with a vengeance
My perfection,
& my queen

Matthew Nino Azcuy was born on 1994 in Olney, a small town in Maryland, USA where he and his family still reside. He is the author of "Views & Haikus", "The Seeker", "The Lion Kicks", "Matthew Nino Azcuy", and "My Castle" published by Adelaide Books (to be released in November). Writing poems is Matthews passion; and his work consists of a spiritual, romantic, and motivational nature. All works available on Amazon.com.

Grip Death

By Ryan Kovacs

How do you live with a terminal disease?
The answer is simple:

you don't— you die with it.

That was my mentality upon hearing my diagnosis
that I had only a few months to live.

5 to be exact
and that was with
4 months of suffering. Which only left
3 weeks until I'd feel
residual effects of longevity treatment 2 days a week
that made
1 hour seem like an eternity.

The sickness
it's sickening in and of itself and yet it is more alive than I.
It thrives off my life takes
and takes and takes

like some tax collector who's never satisfied with your debt.

I don't know exactly what it was that allowed me this
opportunity to have my very being extracted away from me
as if I were a wooden floor being stripped
then sanded down until I was rough
and in need of application that would
somehow beautify my outlook on life.

It took awhile
to understand the meaning

and significance of such an event when hearing the words
"not long to live"
was the same as saying "before long you'll die."

But don't we all know that?

Surely we will all die
but seldom do we have a clock to watch
as time slips away from us
like a bar of soap in the shower
as we attempt to cleanse ourselves of regrets and sins
we know we can't make up or take back.

And while I approach the end I find my
regrets are stacking like bricks in a wall
building a tomb in which I will be confined to
as I recall pastimes

that replay like old VHS tapes constantly needing
to be rewound before they enter the sleeve
of memory they once came from.

Titles of moments
both significant and meaningless that lure my inner thoughts
like a moth to a flame until I catch fire from
the meandering mundane.

Yet
here I sit
in a tranquil state
reminiscing childhood anthologies of laughter and play
as I gaze into the younger eyes of my children
whom have much more grasped the concept of my demise
but don't play into juvenile behavior displayed by yours truly.

It is in those pure imperfect times that time itself is expressed

via a nervous tick
which presents itself as a tell pressuring my body
to act on it's own
out of fear of the unknown and terror of the known.

Because it is death that I fear what it will do to me
once I've passed on bereft of life
and
ceasing to be.
When Shakespeare asked "to be or not to be?"

He failed to acknowledge what do we become?

I have been a being
of formed skin and bone that has
transmogrified transgressed and transitioned
a simply complex life and yet
I have become a being
of decaying cells and muscle that has
regressed redirected and resolved
a complexly simple existence.

And that's all I will ever be— a speck in
the human race a blip on the map
a particle among the stars with nothing to define me
nor remember my name and what I stood for
what I believed in what I dreamt of what I achieved.
Because there is no place

for me for you for us for them
among the vastness we claim to know
because the unknown is greater
and holds more keys
to paths we've barely begun to seek.
It is there that we all will find the answers
to questions we never imagined or dared to
ask because reality was never ours.

What we claim to own
is but a loan to the universe

and upon our demise we are cashed in in order to
behold the true wonders which are unable to be
seen heard smelled touched felt believed.
And it is there
at the brink of death
that I see the line everyone must cross to never
truly know what is beyond and infinite
where
both knowledge and wisdom
are but the stepping stones towards boundless possibilities
of what was what is
and
what could have been.

I see it now
the obscure light demanding recourse
in the direction of endless space where time is neither
an enemy or friend
but a guide down a tunnel
that gathers the pieces of infinity and pushes them
together creating a resemblance of myself that is both
recognized and foreign placing him before me

and challenging everything the universe can conceive.

I reach out
making acquaintances with a version of my mind
body and soul
grasping the hand

that pulls me from then to here
to now until I fade

fade
fade
fade
fade…

Ryan A. Kovacs has been writing for about 18 years now having self-published 3 books of poetry and a poetry ebook on Amazon. He has taken creative writing and poetry classes in college and developed his own style while following the flow of novels-in-verse.

Black-Eyed Susan

By Patrick Erickson

A sometimes upright annual
with alternating basal leaves
and stout branching stems
covered by course hair
hence brown Betty
It has daisy-like flowers
with yellow ray-florets
compassing brown or black
dome-shaped disc-florets
thus yellow ox-eye daisy
The genus name Rudbeckia
honors Olaus Rudbeck
a botany professor
at the University of Uppsala
and one of Linnaeus's teachers
Look for the flowerheads
in late summer and early autumn
Look for them in Maryland
where they are designated the state flower
Look for a blanket of them

around the winner's neck
at the Preakness Stakes
The roots of the black-eyed Susan
are an astringent
a wash for sores
a poultice for snake bites
an infusion for colds
and worms in children
a diuretic
and eardrops for earaches
Butterflies are drawn to them
in large color-masses.

Patrick Theron Erickson, a resident of Garland, Texas, a Tree City, just south of Duck Creek, is a retired parish pastor put out to pasture himself. His work has appeared in *Grey Sparrow Journal, Cobalt Review*, and *Burningword Literary Journal*, among other publications, and more recently in *Adelaide Literary Magazine, The Main Street Rag, Tipton Poetry Journal, Right Hand Pointing*, and *Danse Macabre*.

Last Beating

By Peter Freeman

Where is he? He should be here,
and dinner is almost ready.
He's late, he's very late,
I'm tense and need to be steady.
A bird, A bird, I found a bird,
the wing, it looks so bent.
The eyes, so black, so small,
look at me from heaven sent.
It's dark outside, so very dark,
I remember the great big chest.
I was trapped, I could not leave,
my cousin, on the lid he pressed.
In my arms, I carried it gently,
its feathers so soft and smooth.
A home for it, I hoped to find,
its trauma I wished to sooth.
The dinner ready, the family called,
all save one was sat.
My face a-fire and skin all taut,
oh where, oh where is he at!

Through the town, I walked and walked,
looking to find some one.
My little bird, so very quiet now,
was looking completely stunned.
He must be near, he's got to be near,
I cannot have him gone.
Am I to blame, and did I fail,
a mother to my first-born son.
Under the streetlight, my poor bird
lay still, its heart had stopped.
I turned it over with gentle care,
but its little head just dropped.
I must find him, where's my coat?
Out in the dark I strode.
I called and called, my voice now hoarse,
echoing down the road.
In the sand, I dug a hole,
and placed its feathered shape.
So perfect, yet without the spark,
from Death, it did not escape.
I feel the rage, my impotence raw,
I had to take some action.
Back to the house, I went reluctant,
to eat my meal in distraction.
The moonlit mound revealed a tale
that only I could read.
I straightened up and headed home,
and lateness gave me speed.
I can't take it, I must stand up,

my heart it beat so hard.
Fists are clenched, I break my cup,
a finger cut from shard.
I see the lights all aglow,
home it made me feel.
Through the door, I quickly flowed
into warmth and light and meal.
He's here, he's here!
I feel my rage within.
My self control now disappears,
and I am my evil twin.
Her eyes burn dark and very deep,
and face becomes a mask.
That look I know, my fear it leaps,
and I know what soon she'll ask.
"All this night, where have you been!"
I hear my voice so strange.
My devilled twin could be so mean,
as I felt my self to change.
"A bird! A bird! I found a bird!"
I cried in deep despair.
"I gave it help, but it had not stirred,
in spite of all my prayers."
I felt the stick with my grasp,
a broken piece of broom.
I yelled so loud, my voice a rasp,
as I dragged him to the room.
A change had come from somewhere strange,
I had never known this calm.

In all the times of violent exchange,
there never was a balm.
With every blow I rained on him,
I told him of his sin.
I beat him hard from limb to limb,
which made a fearful din.
From far away, I looked with truth,
at the boy that I once was.
And in his place, stood a youth
with a heart of noble cause.
Through rage I knew, there was a wrong,
he did not squirm and scream.
I saw him stand so very strong,
and saw his self-esteem.
I did not feel the stick so hard,
nor the bruise and welts so many.
For steady as a palace guard,
I stood my ground as any.
Through my craze, I saw my ill,
and knew that I was taken.
He had broken me of all my will.
and had left me so forsaken.
I watched the stick slip from her hand,
to clatter on the floor.
I knew that this was not her plan,
for I had robbed her of her chore.
With guilt and shame and confusion plain,
I left him in his world.
With dragging steps in so much pain,

I felt my spirit whirl.
I was transformed, and knew I'd won,
but at such a terrible loss.
Nevermore would we have fun,
but she not be my boss.
At the table, I sat so stunned,
a feeling I did not know.
I missed the bond, now I was shunned,
it added to my woe.
A day had passed, and life moved fast,
it carried on as before.
Yet my life was fresh, a new die cast,
with my soul uplifted and a-soar.

Peter Freeman started writing short stories while in high school and, in his late teens, discovered that poetry gave him an outlet for his emerging feelings. He became passionate about the social, environmental and relationship issues of his youth and found writing was an ideal medium to share his growing concern and solutions for a better world. When Peter uses poetry to tell his stories, he chooses the best medium and style to engage and affect his readers. His powerful adventures are expressed as rhythmical ballads, whimsical pieces are formed using gentle rhymes, and dark verses use heavy overtones to build a strong connection with readers. His short stories are ideas that deliver messages of hope, sadness, conflict, and many other aspects of being human. He draws on the essence of his experiences in the grip of adventure.

Emergence

By Angela Shepherd

Oak and incense meet me at the door. I have come in search of sustenance, a pilgrim. My fingers run gently over the smooth wooden pew as I soak in this divine sensibility, my heart touches divinity. Whispers of spirits desperate and hopeful rise and dance among the golden chandeliers. I bow down, complete in the simplicity of mortal transgressions. Vapors of reserve and release now surround as I step into the innermost void. I welcome the cool breeze that roll through the open window as it beckons memories that have long hidden themselves beneath heavy blankets of disguise.

What was void and once abandoned and bare, is now welcoming and clear. Neither deprived nor drained, but challenged to welcome the clean slate. What was once empty and lacking possesses a shimmering silver lining of freedom, uncharged to choose, stretch and move. Need no longer threatens or haunts as I stand sure footed in the clearing. Hallowed ground holds me now, in shelter of your holy presence.

Beckon me forward now with grace and purpose, breathe new life into me slow and warm with your breath. Give oh unto me your mercy both expansive and small enough to hold here in my hand; a prayer. Dispel the past from the present yet abide, rooted in its brave account. Divine grace within and without full of urgency and promise for your love, as you are, as am I.

Angela Shepherd lives on Cape Cod, MA where she raised her three sons Colby, Myles, and Noah. She has always been creatively inspired by mother nature's sandy beaches and New England's glorious mountains. She has worked in a treatment center helping women build recovery foundations for over 22 years which invigorates her passion for life and hope. A strong faith and confidence in the process of change has infused her writing over the years. She just completed her first book of essays entitled Fierce Recovery, a Call to Rise.

Addiction

By Ross Hardy

I fear that you might be right.
That I have an addictive personality.
That some of the things I do,
are, in fact, some sort of demons
that control my life with their finger
constantly hanging over the self-destruct button.

Could you love this alcoholic though
if I only got drunk on the love that you gave me?
If I did shot after shot of your sensitive spirit,
and drank every last drop of your merlot lip kisses.
Getting wasted and bingeing as I do on your sweet soul.
Would that be ok?

Could you love me if I was an addict
but I only got high on the kisses from you?
Doing line after line
of your gorgeous, sexy body?
What if I was addicted to the high we have when
we are in each others arms after making love,

and our bodies are lifeless and comatose,
and I was fiending for it all the fucking time.
And I took the feeling and injected it into my arm.
hell, I'd give a fuck less if I overdosed.

Could you love me if I was a gambler
but I only gambled on you and I?
All in, against the odds, betting everything
that I have and own that our future
would turn up a winner. Knowing that if not,
if it didn't, and the hands of chance and fate
decided against us,
that we would both lose everything.
I'd still take that bet every time.
Does that make me wrong?

You see, or maybe you don't,
an addictive personality is only
as negative as the connotation.
Addiction is such an ugly word for something
that can actually be so beautiful.
And of all of the habits that I have
there is one that I cannot give up,
that no amount of rehab could
ever help me get through,
and it's the one that is being so lucky
as to be hopelessly addicted to you.

Pastel Painting

By Barbara Bottner

My neighbor, Richie almost never discusses his mother,
Caitlyn O'Neill.
If she was a painting, she'd be pastel.
It's like her outline is blurred.
She floats like a Chagall, a beautiful Irish Chagall.
If I drew her I'd do it in a dark pencil,
making heavy Braque outlines
so you could see her more clearly,
bring her back down to earth,
down to her life here in the Bronx,
so she could help her children.
Lustrous green eyes, thin, elegant face.
A person you'd probably see everyday
walking the streets of Dublin.
I'd make her into a formidable presence.
Someone who could hold the family together.
Because Richie's dad is a dish-flinger,
a wall-puncher.

I wonder if they have any plates left
to eat off of in that house.
Or if there's a draft escaping in every room.
through every wounded wall.

Song Changes

By Emily Brummett

They would go to the bar
every week after work,
to "Karaoke Thursday".
Together.

After graduating,
she moved in with him:
each drowning in eight years
of student loans,
ready to start their lives.

She knew he started going more,
"a regular" status
while she was only invited
on Thursdays

She was fed up
with his excuses and
the way he'd come back-
fingers and mouth

stained Marlboro
and jeans acid-washed Bud Light.

So now,
on Karaoke Thursdays,
she's in the apartment watching Late Night,
while he's swaying left to right,
singing "Don't Stop Believing,"
a beer in hand,
gulping whiskey neats
between song changes and bathroom breaks.

She envisioned their lives together:
Marriage, kids, white-picket-fences
Prolonging her decision to leave, but

she walks out without any argument
on his hangover,
because he was running late
to his daily five-dollar bottomless drafts
and spark of an unfiltered open-mic.

Emily Brummett is a young and aspiring international business entrepreneur who enjoys traveling and writing in her free time. She was published in the Adelaide Literary Magazine No. 14. and is greatly obliged to her friends and family for their endless support.

And So I Believe

By Clark Holtzman

A stranger stood next to me at the city zoo. I had stopped at an exhibit of sand and boulders, limbs and brush. It appeared to be unoccupied. The stranger studied the exhibit intently, nodding his head back and forth as though trying to catch a glimpse of something. The stranger said that you had to stand very still and look carefully but still you might not see the inhabitant of that savannah-like world. He said few people had ever seen one, invisibility being its natural defense against predators, but it was always there. So if one looked hard enough . . . The stranger said the creature's scientific name was Semper absents, which made perfect sense to me. I stood very still, searching the recesses and the deep shadows for signs of the beast. Suddenly my mother, who had been listening nearby, said, "How cruel! Fooling a small boy like that! You should be ashamed of yourself!" She grabbed me by the arm and began to drag me away. The stranger, whoever he was, had vanished when I turned back to look for him. It was as if he had never been there. I thought I caught a glimpse of something among the boulders as my mother hurried me off to the next exhibit (of a family of gnus, I recall), a pair of bright eyes from out of the shadows. I thought I heard a voice whisper, believe.

Clark Holtzman lives in Chapel Hill, North Carolina. Thanks to 2River View, Antiphon (UK), The Madras Mag (India), One, Verse-Virtual, West Trade Review, and The North American Review for recent or forthcoming publications of poems by the author.

Defenestration

By Daisy Bassen

A door makes sense.
The walls and roof make inside
But the door makes it whole
Even as the frame, the hinges break.
The sky recedes and becomes heaven,
The ground needs to be swept.
A door is practical, helpful, a door is Martha
Filling the bowls with sweetmeats, dates, nard.
Windows are an invention some regret.
Only an entrance for thieves and sneaks,
Hands dragging nature, neighbors up to the glass,
The oiled paper, the air that gives in and out
Like breath. Windows are also for murder
But we cannot do without them.
    We all want a view,
A book we can hold before we learn to read.

Daisy Bassen is a psychiatrist in private practice, a wife, mother and a poet. She graduated from Princeton University magna cum laude with a degree in English. Since she graduated from medical school, Daisy published a few poems and in 2016, and was a semi-finalist in the Vassar Miller Prize for Poetry. She lives in Rhode Island with my husband and three children.

Doxology

By Riley Bounds

The hillside child
stands hanging on
every pulse
of clouds,
mouthing
the language
of lightning.
This is
the Ur Text;
this is
the Father
of Nations,
though the child
doesn't know
the name.
Thunder's heartbeat
throngs through
the arteries
of arroyos,
the ventricles

of canyons
below him
and breathes
on the fluid
morphemes
of rivers.
See the child
now greatly alone,
looking
to the stars
caroling
cosmic,
the cuneiform
of constellations
and the
tiny thunder
of his ribcage
proffered
to
Who he does not
know
from the textless
hymnal
of his solar
plexus,
the liturgy
of bone
and marrow.
What can he
say?

Dandelions die;
even the prayers
of birds
get caught
up
in the
stratosphere.

The child raises
a hand
to the sun
softly burning
in the celestial
cathedral,
the moon
in
transit
menorah,
and extends
friendship
to the unknown
Known,
the Painter
of the primordial
acrylic
so textured
as
to be
alive.

Riley Bounds was raised in Alex, Oklahoma. He earned a BA in Creative Writing from the University of Central Oklahoma and is currently pursuing an MA in Philosophy from Talbot School of Theology. He plans to do doctoral work in theology. He resides in La Mirada, California.

I Am My Own Army

By Emily Eigenheer

My name is not singular,
It is not a single entity,
Rather a collection of names that have
been acquired over time.
I come from two very different people,
The wolf and the lamb.
I am strong,
I am my own army.

I love the funky old rhythms of the 60's,
And the feeling of animals' fur as it brushes against my skin.
I used to think that conformity was the way to success,
And that unique wasn't unique,
And being weird was undesirable.
Now I realize conformity breeds contempt,
Even more so than familiarity.
I know now that I am me,
And there will never be another me,
Because I am my own army.

I was told that being a nerd was not a bad thing,
And that my last name was more than an
unpronounceable jumble of letters.
I discovered that Eigenheer actually means something,
I discovered that it meant 'own army'.

I am a scorpion,
But a lion lives inside me.
My sting can be deadly,
But it is always well-deserved.
I am strong both mentally and physically,
I am not afraid to speak my views nor to
argue with the views of others.
I have deep brown eyes that hide a tornado of thoughts,
But I live in the eye of the storm.

If my hands could talk,
They would say feel everything.
Let it all in and hold nothing back.
Touch the plants and animals that surround you,
Run your fingers over the skin of the people you love,
And realize that your hands belong to you and no one else.

My forehead reads own army,
And my heart is fueled by a raging fire.
That fire fuels the war brewing inside of me,
Struggles versus remedies,
Society versus Individuality,
Me versus Them.

It doesn't matter the battle,
Nor the two combatants,
All that matters is that one of them is me,
Fighting for myself and no one else,
Because I am my own army.

Emily Eigenheer is currently a college sophomore in Sacramento, CA where she is preparing to transfer to a nursing school. She writes poetry, short stories, and fiction recreationally but plans to one day write professionally. In addition to writing, she paints, draws, and knits.

Calligraphy

By Sarah Snyder

I slant the bevel of the point
to a forty-five degree angle,

move the pen across the page,
gliding winged

against a clouded sky,
black feathered and smooth.

A pen fuels, catalogues
the lines and curves,

the curl of a wave.
We were once water.

What did we know
before we could write?

Ocean Days

By Talon Florig

In a lot of ways you taught me the ocean.
Sure, I've always known how to swim
But waves
East coast sunset
Seagull sand prints, triangle shaped.
For the first time in my life
I want to walk out to sea
And let the ocean take me
Because dying now is dying happy
I imagine you are Earth
And I swim in your waters
And you massage my tired
Soul.
Salt water healing draught
Tincture of tenderness
I drink you up
And go mad

Talon Florig is a poet and painter from Lancaster, PA with
a tool kit full of blunt metaphors and destructive memories.

Counter Naratives

By Shirley Jones-Luke

There was no slavery that's why they tell us to get over it. No need for reparations for an event that never happened. No need to identify the thousands of unmarked graves of African men, women and children buried across the South. They weren't killed for escaping, resisting or speaking against fictional masters. They weren't hung, whipped, dragged or raped. No lynchings. No strange fruit swinging in the breeze. Today's America doesn't believe that we are traumatized by a history that never existed. White Americans think we are making things up. Making excuses. Lazy. Ungrateful. Africans were treated as workers in the new economy that valued their labor. They were a part of America's rise as a world power and honored for their service. Our people were always equal never separated. A misunderstanding. White America wanted black families to be together in their own neighborhoods to foster community. White saviors. There was no need to come into white neighborhoods because black neighborhoods had all that they needed. But if they did come into white neighborhoods they were welcomed with open arms, smiling eyes and helping hands. Who would burn crosses on the lawns of Black families? What is a negro? A colored? A nigger? White Americans would never use such language to describe blacks. Ridiculous! Even further, to tell black Americans to go back to Africa? Never! Your African ancestors were invited here, built this country and remained. Black Americans act as if they had overstayed their welcome. Perish the thought! Black America, this is your country too. Those white hoods we wore were our faces.

Shirley Jones-Luke is a poet and a writer. Ms. Luke lives and writes in Boston, Massachusetts. She was a 2016 Watering Hole Poetry Fellow. Her work has been published by ENUF, Fire Poetry and Deluge.

Tulip Tree

By Gloria Monaghan

The purple salvia started up in the border garden today
along with the white and blue morning glories;
they occupy my mind.

I see the hammock every day and think
about when you and I laid down
you faced me and I faced the tulip tree above
we weren't thinking

about after or before.
Somehow the small pink and red roses
started to rebloom.

I figure no one told them summer is ending.
Instead, I think about how those small
flowers just come up out of nowhere

uninvited and adored.

Gloria Monaghan is a Professor of Humanities at Wentworth Institute in Boston. She has two books of poetry, Flawed (Finishing Line Press, 2011) and The Garden (Flutter Press 2015). Her poems have appeared in Blue Max Review, 2River, Adelaide, Aurorean, Aries, among others. She currently lives on the South Shore of Boston with her daughters.

At The Office Window

By Lowell Jaeger

Solitary runner in a far chaotic expanse
of dried timothy and wild rye, wending his way
uphill, huffing white puffs of dream, climbing
November's inexhaustible frigid morning air.

Now, he nears the summit – soon to crest the rise –
and will I lose sight of whatever held me, attracted
my gaze, attuned my receptors, as I attended
his progress, marked his strain and determination?

He's gone. A lonely wind follows, fanning the grass
in flattened zigzags, while a parade of ragged
clouds trudges overhead, onward, looking down
on the big-wide world, lifting my thoughts

to sail skyward after that solitary runner, wherever
he's arrived, one step chasing the next, each
moment linked, each heartbeat, each of us joined
invisibly, a certain rhythm and flow, so intricate

and vast, so easily passed over, so difficult to name.

Lowell Jaeger (Montana Poet Laureate 2017-2019) is founding editor of Many Voices Press and recently edited New Poets of the American West, an anthology of poets from eleven western states. Lowell has taught writing classes at numerous conferences and workshops and is currently Professor of English/ Creative Writing at Flathead Valley Community College (Kalispell, Montana), where he also serves as Humanities Division Chair. He is a graduate of the Iowa Writer's Workshop, winner of the Grolier Poetry Peace Prize, and recipient of fellowships from the National Endowment for the Arts and the Montana Arts Council. Lowell was awarded the Montana Governor's Humanities Award for his work in promoting civil civic discourse. He is the author of eight collections of poems, the most recent of which are Or Maybe I Drift Off Alone (Shabda Press 2016) and Earth-blood & Star-shine (Shabda Press 2018).

The Legend Of Chaos

By Deanna M. Lehman

I remember when it started
Violently into existence.
A mutant man-made needle
Slithered silver screams
Into my dreams of consciousness.
Opening my eyes to a land
Of compromising colors and unconditional time.
I can't remember my name game same shame blame.
Just a flash crash wave of white wonder
Distant thunder black blood blundered
Wanderlust for dimensions of unparalleled symmetry
A cemetery of sanctity
Of downcast dreams and grating gleams.

Staring at the drab gray walls
Which stalls then falls and crawls.
There I saw my nemesis
Within the melted dismembered mists
And chaos was my game.

To look into its depthless eyes
That cries and lies, denies and ties.
I felt the falling foundation
Of humiliated humanity.
I see I see
Its conscious coil
Of twisted turmoil
And sardonic society
Sadistically soiled
By the petulance of its purity.
So free in it's fluidity.
Sitting by warm window sills
A chill a thrill and silence still.
It's memory has scarred by heart
In knowing night
I deemed to fight
And merrily murder memories
In lash, flash, slash, ash ash
And chaos is my game.

I went into the scented chapel
In which to grapple hand to fist
The blistered burn of childhood.
The tattered tremors of yesterday
Which plays and strays today.
Kissing comfort coldly aside
The faces forgot to make me cry.
The faces forgot that they had lied
And I forgot they tried.

I gave a grateful goodbye
To those too shy to fly.
I dove in drowning dreaming
To taunted trauma and silenced screaming.
Kissing sucking fucking streaming
Tears of time, sublime unseeming.
Pondered parts of panicked pleading
Bleeding needing feeding
Laughing crying dying sigh.
Embalmed embered ecstasy
And I remember, I remember
Who's to blame in shame
Of shadowed sorrows and obscenities
And chaos was my name.

Deanna M. Lehman is an author and poet currently re-
siding in West Union, WV. She has been the creator and editor-in-chief of two zines called Pandora's Box and Lollygag.
Has performed spoken word for the Saturn Series Poets of
NYC under director Su Polo and has a poetry chapbook out
called Morphine Moonbeams. Deanna also recently debuted
her autobiographical book, Kinderwhore, currently available
through Amazon.

Sunday Oranges

By Manuel Madera

The gilt bells toll
Early, early Sunday morning—
The children, incorruptible, stroll
Along the strand, undiscerning.

A thought ascends
The throat with most thirst,
While the children descend
The stairs to lead first.

Forbidden fruits are known
To lurk, to hide—
The loquacious child and his herd
In this story they bide.

It is an orchard;
A grove, perhaps—
It seemed thoughtful torture
Broods are unable to grasp.

"The Orange in the Welkin,"
It has been called.
It is unwelcome,
It is rather appalled.

Following a ripe scent-
A sweet, heavenly pleasure—
Wandering wherever it went
As if it were infinite treasure.

But the trek tired the Orange
As he is swift to fall.
The forbidden orange
Has been a tale too tall.

A bit crestfallen, they venture back
To the stairs, to the strand—
The night is said to turn black,
Enveloping the pebbles and sand.

Sunday oranges, like gold,
Are foolishly sought—
The children, of course, slumber untold
Of these Sunday oranges that easily rot.

Manuel Madera and his poetry emerge from the dreary environs of the world, steadily ascending the ladder of prominence and success. Jumping from pseudonym to pseudonym, Madera gathers the world around him and turns it into a world, or several, of his own.

Why We Don't Pray Anymore

By Rafiki Chemari

Is it Saint Paul?
Is it Saint John?
Is it Saint Matthew?
Or, is it Saint Christopher?
(No one knows anymore)
When it's the Roman Catholic Church…
That is quietly harboring
Such a dirty little secret!

Whether it's the archdiocese in Boston,
Or the one that is located
In Augusta, Georgia.
Now the spotlight is on…
The entire state of Pennsylvania,
And good-ole' Father Pedophilia.
Why couldn't they just arrest him!
Or, the hundreds and hundreds of countless others?

The cover-up is tremendous!
But rather than acknowledge

This gargantuan problem...
That might tarnish the sanctimonious image
That the vatican has so falsely created.
They continue to appear to be...
Seemingly sinless and so superior to all
While the boys' lives are ruined and they take the fall.

But now as a politically driven adult
Who is actively lobbying
As a democrat to revoke!
For it is written that:
"It is the one who reluctantly
 'Broke bread and drank wine'
With the priestly perpetrators of his youth...
That one day rebelled at the eucharist feast!"

Ms. Rafiki Chemari is a native San Francisco resident. She is a local member of THE SCREEN ACTORS GUILD and ASCAP Music Publishing and she currently has a music track on hold for placement in a feature film with ONE NITE STAND MUSIC. In February 2018 she was an Adelaide Voices Best Essay Award Finalist for "Women in Prison" and it was included in the special issue of the: ADELAIDE VOICES AN-THOLOGY 2018 VOLUME TWO

Coward's Way

By Nathan Tracy

Never to forget that awful
collapse, domino-effect
of floor falling through floor
into a mountain of steel
and pulverized ash. First
the North Tower, then
the South. Thousands, you
guessed, descending at
the speed of sound— a spire
sinking like the mast of
a great ship into a sea of soot.
How staged it seemed,
so fantastically surreal.
The incomparable blue
of a perfect Tuesday sky
the unlikeliest backdrop
of catastrophe. What looked
like a computer generated
hoax, manipulation of
absurdity in hi-def— too

heartrending to be real.
As hard to fathom as my
own death. This world,
sometimes, mordantly
inscrutable. A nation stunned
over and over again into
awe, hatred and remorse.
I drank deeply— mind-numbing,
copious amounts. A coward's way,
you could say, of dealing
with the day.

Tony Tracy is the author of two collections of poetry, The Christening and Without Notice. His work is forthcoming or has recently appeared in Flint Hills Review, North American Review, Poetry East, Hotel Amerika, Potomac Review and various other magazines and journals.

The Forest

By Maureen Grace

The forest pulled its curtain back today,
and swooning May enticed me to explore
its radiant tapestry, bade me stray
deep in greening patterns threading its floor.
A path I knew or thought I did drew me
to a cabin by the water, shuttered;
a family's pride abandoned hastily;
a doll, a tiny truck, their hopes gutted.
What sad fortune left these dear toys behind,
sandy testaments to small disasters?
Could I but change this bleak tale with my mind
Might my orphaned dreams seed newborn masters?
The forest shelters all who seek its shade,
holding visions and those that come unmade.

Maureen Grace has been writing stories and poems all her life but has only now begun to send them out for publication. Her short story, *Dagger*, appeared recently in the July edition of *Adelaide Literary Magazine*. Maureen has a master's in literature and had won numerous awards for her writing in television, film and print advertising.

Rising Action

By Sara Pridmore Bailey

I wonder how my skin doesn't scorch you
As you cradle my face in your hands. I wonder
If you can hear my blood rush. You brush your
Thumb across my bottom lip, and I forget to
Breathe. This is as bold as you've ever been.
Your eyes brim with unspoken thoughts that
I wait for you to spill. We both know it's hard
For me, and you too clearly fill the strain. Held in
Your gaze, your intensity makes me shiver,
Makes me sweat. Then you remember that this
Is not where you belong, and you drop your eyes.
Inertia is exhausting. I feel its weight, but I long
To feel yours. Lips pressed together, eyes shut tight,
You bite your lip instead of mine. With a pained
Half-smile and a rueful look, you let your hands fall,
And you step back. I want to reach out and stop you;
It's only a crime if we get caught. But we both know
The sin still stains. Disappointed and relieved, I watch
You walk away. Then, I remember to breathe.

Sara Bailey received her B.A. in Writing and Rhetoric from the University of Central Arkansas and her MFA in Creative Writing with an emphasis in fiction from Murray State University. The majority of her writing is fiction or poetry, but she has also tried her hand at nonfiction and screenwriting. Her work has been published in New Madrid and Torrid Literature Journal, and her poetry will be included in the fall edition of Big Muddy.

Windows

By Sam James

You stare, I want to go.
I nod towards the window.
Inside, the rain and the dark
distort our reflections.

Outside, it's welcome;
all the things we've ever said and done
echo with the drops.

Two drunks hold their heads,
laughing at us from up the road.
You want to put a stop to that.

You say, if I could only have a garden it'd be a breath of air.

I think about crisp flowers blown clean off towards the sea
and say, I'm glad I made my life myself.

Nothing makes me feel so poor
as remembering out loud to you

when I didn't have a house.

Nothing makes us feel more sick
than wishing we could be rich
and not have to worry about laughing drunks
and places we don't want to be.

You say it all so we agree:

we can't stay now,
sometimes, there were no windows,
one day there might've been something else.

Sam James is a new writer from the north of England, and has been published in the following online poetry magazines: *Allegro, London Grip, Peeking Cat, Clockwise Cat, and Ink, Sweat and Tears.*

Dare to Whisper the F-Word

Tinka Harvard

We are quiet, gentle in speaking, whispers really,
while quiet motions are delicate in touch. Tender
and soft, warm too, as honey, on a summer's day.

Love's delicious and joy-filled, midnight in mystery,
and mornings too… serendipitous and silent.

Lovely, lyrical, still quiet and quaking.
Sweet. Intimate. Intense.

We dare to whisper the f-word. Fluid in flow, dripping in
desire, this morning, in midst of morning meditations…
tender in touch, taste, delicious, and soothing in need. This
morning, love's slippery in silken sheets, and sheer sweetness.

We dare to taste a tiny bit more, before we
open the curtains, and open the bedroom door,
and wake the children, before school.

Tinka Harvard is an author and theologian. She is a graduate of Wagner College and has a master's in divinity from Union Theological Seminary at Columbia University in New York City. She is the author of Lush Life, a collection of short stories published in 2018 by Adelaide Books. Her writings have appeared most recently in publications including Adelaide Literary Magazine, Adelaide Voices Anthology 2018, StepAway Magazine, and Polychrome Ink. To learn more, please visit www.tinkaharvard.com.

Passing Creek Road

By Tina Weikert

On Creek Road the phlox has
sprung up from the walnut black bottom.
It's cotton candy plumes,
denying it could be a weed,
continue to shake sweetness upon the creek:
a sugarplum breeze that
can eclipse all else with
just one dazzling breath.
It would be so easy to lie down there
among clouds of pink and white for a turn;
to ardently accept their summons
as if they were a royal poppy field
emblazed all cinnabar and snuff;
their enticement dazzlingly convincing.
I'm certain the phlox would beam and
raise their petals up in startled,
blooming honor, but for today
the dusk of afternoon presses on
and I can grant no dignity by stopping.
In their mind, this makes them no less a flower.
In my mind, this makes me no less a poet.

Tina Weikert loves print and photography equally. She has found the best way to combine her two passions is by contributing articles with accompanying photos to her local newspaper. She has been known to eat handfuls of orange circus peanuts while doing so. Visit her at: any-given-moment.blogspot.com. Photography forthcoming in Edify Publications LLC.

Super 8

By Timothy Muren

Your grave, Phil Silver, should be here:
Philip's Fill-Up—Gas and Gro. Hilarious, bro.
Filled up with bones like a new Christian,

like a new Big-Wheel coasting to dirt, down
steep on plastic, breaking apart against torque
and narrow concrete. Ghosts, remember,

sleeping between liquor store and University,
staring up at dandelions growing along plum creek's edge
to hang over us. No old photos spark you, Philemon,

only the heavy swing of coiled guitar cables,
linking deep to deep, as S-street linked Super-8
to Roadrunner. Could you place in memory--stucco

corners, in-through-the-out-door back-lot-stealth,
horrible suites, Shoney's breakfast abutment,
restaurant row. I do not know how or why

we stopped. How long did I wait for you above
Alsopp ball-fields, missing your input on a ref
calling time. A transient camp under interstate.

Barefoot kids in a truck-bed staring back
through jangling. Truckers curbing rigs. Ring-tones
rigged to hang from paunchy trucker belts.

Hitch that rig, Philip McGroin, let us set sail,
Docker's pockets bulging, trailers listing left
across this great land, yours and mine. A few precarious
corners, a few more miles, please, before I lose you.

Tim Muren lives and works in Little Rock, Arkansas. Tim has published poems in *Prairie Schooner, Confrontation, Cortland Review,* and others.

Leah's Kaleidoscope

By Jeffrey Kass

You have the depth of the Mariana Trench
Humor of a Hyena. Laughing. Laughing.
Laughing. Deep belly laughs

You anger like Katrina crashing on the shores of an
already poor community, as if that doesn't matter. And
sometimes you create the distance of the Darian Gap

Your beauty rivals the Cliffs of Moher
Longing with the heart of the Asiatic Lion

Wrath like a thousand suns
With your sometimes sadness of Jeanne d'Arc

Yet you grow and grow and grow, as if a strong
Baobab tree, living for hundreds of years
Intelligence of vos Savant

But you tantrum like a summer storm
And cover with the coldness of Verkhoyansk

Then you shine, more than the light of
Venus in a late September sky
The brilliance of the roundest diamond

Your claws of the Harpy Eagle hurt so much
With itchiness of Hogweed

But then your wisdom reaches beyond the Oracle of Delphi
Something so special about you, as if you were
the first child born to a new mother

Bitter as the taste of White Dandelions
Sometimes sharp like Cutco. Ouch!

You emerge, though, loving as the Aries zodiac
Faithful as the Yellow Crusted Penguin

Analytical as Curie
And so judging as one of seventy in the Sanhedrin

Affectionate and touching. Sensual
Amazingly alluring as a Windsor Beauty

Pain of a first degree burn
The trauma of a broken heart, that has been with you so long

Heal, beautiful Leah, and let the soulful
mosaic of the life in you flourish
You are like no other. Wouldn't want you to be

The Tubbs Fire

By T. William Wallin

The evacuation started at 430 in the morning
while we were somewhere south of Chicago
36,000 feet in the air, absent of toxic fumes
fully present of manufactured air
Traveling to New York City, about
as far east as you can get away from the disaster
we heard of the news while on a train
gliding over the Hudson, causing sparks to shoot
off the tracks like wild embers void of intent

What happened to our neighborhood?
the one we shared our first studio the size of a shoebox,
but the amount of memories created
couldn't even fit into a redwood warehouse
The town where we first met, awkward conversations
shared between puffs of work-break cigarettes
next to back parking lot dumpsters
Learning about each other, our favorite musicians
and worst drunken experiences
shedding our vulnerability and exposing all fears

we didn't fall in love in that town
we just remembered we always were

the warm rain the size of thick melancholy
impressionist brush strokes
fell outside our lower east side apartment
2,500 miles away from 1,500 degree wild fires raging
as psychotic inferno episodes
surrounding our once sleepy town, encased
by forested mountain peaks,
a record dry season now burning the blue away
and casting coal mine explosions into the air
we call every friend and family member we know
hoping the end receiver is picked up
there is nothing we can do on this side
but we have to know
the answer we get back is simply
"paradises are built from hell"